# BRANE MOZETIČ

Translated by Elizabeta Žargi and Timothy Liu

*BODY LANGUAGE 04*

## A MIDSUMMER NIGHT'S PRESS

New York

This book was published with the support of Trubar Foundation
at the Slovene Writers' Association, Ljubljana, Slovenia.

Cover photographs © Massimo Caregnato
http://www.flickr.com/photos/massimocare/

A Midsummer Night's Press
16 West 36th Street
2nd Floor
New York, NY 10018
amidsummernightspress@gmail.com
www.amidsummernightspress.com

Grateful acknowledgments are made to the magazines
and websites where some of these poems,
sometimes in earlier versions, first appeared:
*Blesok, Chroma, Corpus, Melancholia's Tremulous
Dreadlocks, Mirage, Orient Express, Poetry International,
Prague Literary Revue, Savage Poetry Review, Shampoo,
Talisman,* and *Transcript.*

Designed by Marróndediseño www.quintatinta.com

First edition, December 2008.

ISBN-13: 978-0-9794208-3-2
ISBN-10: 0-9794208-3-0

Printed in Spain.
Depósito legal: M-47790-2008

# CONTENTS

**1**

He arrived late, as usual. No grounds
for harmony any longer. Things had become
banal: life, writing, all superfluous.
He lay down next to me, embraced me,
and in that moment I became aware
of a scent. Flinched, checked again,
but nothing. It was clear. I started
to heave, got up and rushed
to the bathroom. Tried to get some air
through an open window, everything
spinning. A man's scent.
The years from which I'd been running
had returned. Was it his scent?
When did it arrive? Had it been here
before? Or was it the scent of another man
on him? He didn't follow me, didn't knock,
but remained there, too far.
I shivered, locked up on the floor.
It didn't help. My stepfather's hand
shot after me, a man's hand,
my head blown off. Each time
he came near, I'd get out of the way
even if the hand was far. The scent

already enough. It was impossible
to get it out of the apartment. I would
step away from men, not liking
their world. Which one did I belong to
now? Did I give off such a scent
when hitting someone else?
How it hurts now. Shall I unlock the door,
shall I wash him? Is it possible? Shall I
bundle up somewhere else and try to fall asleep without him?

## 2

The dog runs about the meadow as I watch.
Every so often he stops, sniffs, runs on.
Goes in circles. Sniffs around the molehills
mostly. Pokes right into them.
I'm distracted by the phone vibrating in my pocket.
I'll be there soon. What are you doing,
asks a well-known poetess. Are you reading? Writing?
It's probably nice in the park. No, no, I get flustered.
I'm watching molehills… and my dog
who's sticking his nose in them. *Oh, really?* I
thought you were working. Well, I'll call you when I
finish. He has now started on the largest one.
He digs furiously, sniffing. I'm too stupid
to write smart poems. I run over to him
because he's overdoing it. I shout, but he pays no

attention. I pull him back, kneel down
next to a tunnel leading to that land
of moles. He's already killed one. Behind,
someone is saving tree-bark in a panic, a tiny
mole-poet putting together his book.
He'll drag it deeper, into the earth, have it
bound and then through thousands of tunnels
it will make its way to the central mole-library
where history is already noted in millions of books.
I smile; once again my pocket's vibrating. So be it.
I get up, move away, the dog watching me, and
when I turn away, he knows that he's allowed
to destroy what remains.


## 3

Why don't I like soldiers? Because they make
children everywhere. Kill children. My best
memory of my father is of the photograph of him
in military uniform. All the rest have faded.
I have no idea where he disappeared, where he is.
I don't remember a single touch. Or I am
terrified by it. At the barracks we'd spend
the whole day walking here and there, cleaning our boots
hundreds of times, without question. Soldiers
always keep the peace. The same way the police

protect us. In uniform, all are somehow
equal. This bores me.
I always imagine empty heads
following a script that is
always the same. I'm afraid most people
have uniforms. Or they are close
to it. And when you once asked me
to put one on, I didn't know
you were trying to brainwash me.
And when you later told me that you
had found a cop, I understood you.
Even at a young age I wasn't any good at playing
Cowboys and Indians. I didn't understand a thing.


**4**


Afraid to pass your house. Always afraid
of you, of your expectations, your
understanding. You were stronger: outbursts,
broken plates, the time you leapt
from the car, screamed lying down in front of the tires:
Go ahead and run me over! It was horrible
under the beams of those headlights. I trembled when
you began coming home late, towards morning. Nerves
would twist under your gaze.
We'd talk for months about accepting each other,

until you had enough and demolished
me with three words. May have been spoken
on purpose, words that linger on
in my head, destroying my affairs. I'm afraid
to pass your house. Where you hammer nails
at night. Into the wall. Into my aching
skull! I would go miles
for you to stop it.
To take back those words.


**5**


What happened? I took
a night-time stroll to some sort of reservation
for the alternative forces from the pathetic nation
to which I belong, and look, I was carried
here and there. In darkness they sipped
beer, talked, yelled, some of them
jumping around wildly on the dance floor.
It stank of weed, two dealers
poked me in the ribs, that I should buy something.
So I said to myself, I might as well stock up a bit,
maybe something nice will come along. I had
already spent half my life trying to
stay alive to perhaps discover the mystery
of life! Now I've wandered off

among the young so that I would forget those
fruitless efforts, and here was a boy
who was only waiting to drug himself
unconscious. I pushed the pill in
his hand and smiled conspiratorially.
I knew that I could not remain
sober. He got higher,
rolling his eyes, grinding his teeth,
and spoke with great difficulty.
He stuck to my heels and our silence
amid head-pounding music
moved me. I don't know how we came
home, but there I was lying next to him.
He slept, night outside, and I
could not fall asleep. So I got dressed,
stepped out between the houses and the streets.
Only then did I realize it was snowing,
the ground covered. I looked up.
Under the beams of the street lamps I saw
snowflakes flying towards me,
everything spinning, so beautiful
that all questions became completely
meaningless.

**6**

People decide these days between war
and peace. The aggressive ones are more in favor
of the former. They wait in long lines and cast their
votes. Others, hunched over in their
shacks, do not understand and have never
understood why they are alive. And I
sit here in front of my own life realizing
how banal it is. Barely worth mentioning.
I am silent. All those books, all that
talk and writing have become lost
in my mind. I no longer know anything. Only
that I'd rather disappear. This nonsense
suddenly hits me as I stand up in front
of my own life, turn around and jump
out. I walk around the town, the shops,
I talk the whole time. About the banal
things that become fun
and put me in a good mood,
words I play with, with meaning, nothing
fateful anymore, nothing tragic,
deciding. Even deciding about war,
religion, or love, everything
has rolled off my chest, swarms somewhere
under my feet, and I smile,
redeemed, worry-free about what will happen

to my banal life that sulks alone
in its room and ponders and ponders.


**7**


That girl is coming again this afternoon. Every
afternoon it's someone else, but she won't leave my head.
A huge pile of catalogues in front of her, mail-order
megamarkets, the lowest prices,
she flips through them with interest. At times
she stops and gives me a glowing look. In pieces,
a small girl comes, crying, holding
herself between her thighs. I ask why. Too many
flashy colors. Models in bras, guys in
sweaters, underwear. She becomes
nervous, skips pages. That's him, she bites her lips,
the one with hairy arms! Then she is at
the laundry detergents that remove
all stains, however old, her story
known. I've heard hundreds just like it.
I look through the window, penetrated by the desire
to have never been born, never begun
nor ended. The worst is the stomach tightening, shortness
of breath, trembling hands. She rearranges the catalogues.
What can I say to her? Does she expect me
to say anything? I ask her what

she'd like to hear. Nothing. I prefer you
to be silent. And once again she leans over catalogues.
I want it all, all of this.

**8**

Friday is the day you think of death. That's why
you have to go out, having had enough
of torment, masochism, constantly
running into walls. You're stoned and drunk
and you drive from club to club. You barely know
who you've been kissing, the faces
foggy. You're tempted to take someone
home, but then you forget.
You get stopped by the police who tell you
you're drunk and must continue on foot.
In madness, your friends drag you to the next
hole where you get even more stoned
and drunk. It's dark. The blinds have been pulled down
so that morning will never come.

**9**

It seems that missiles have lit up the sky. No words
around me. There must be a racket

that I am unaware of, don't hear. I call an expert,
enough books, bodies, for him to find
a point from which everything could start
over. Not much time needed. He lays out a black cover
and orders me to surrender my
nakedness. He puts on black gloves and touches me.
Every so often, he asks if I can feel it,
if anything hurts. Inch by inch,
he sucks me, lies down on me heavily
and bites my ears. I wait for him to find that
spot where the universe opens up and I'm gasping
for air, when I feel as I do lying
next to you, when I put my hand
on your chest and tremble. I can use
a needle, he suggests. I'll prick your
chest, hands, I'll pierce your penis,
some people still enjoy that. What should I say?
Let him use his knowledge, all of his
capabilities, let him somehow bring back
that feeling for a second, a feeling that's been lost.
He doesn't understand. He helps everyone
but I wish for something that does not exist,
something I've made up, something only I can
erase. After hours, he gives up, packs up
his instruments and leaves. My wounds burn,
all that I feel.

**10**

As I sit in a sidewalk cafe, under the sun's first
rays, I still have to wrap myself in a jacket, and it's
spring. A woman holding a child moves between
the tables, stops, stretches her hand out.
A waiter chases her off and people go on
about the newest cars, chicks, clothes.
Not about politics, no one is interested in that anymore,
not to mention philosophical views on the world.
Bottles follow one another, they are lining them up
with broad smiles. A boy walks up to me and
shows me his arms covered in wounds, scars.
We've known each other for years. He sits down. And he just
looks at me. I offer him a cigarette. He smokes calmly
without saying a word. Then he whispers
slyly: you'll like this. He pulls a razor from
his pocket and cuts into the swollen flesh
of his arm. All is bloody in a moment.
Someone screams, the waiter comes running, the boy
stands up, he doesn't need to be pushed away, he smiles at me
and moves on. I feel sharp stares coming
my way, I feel the emptiness of those
conversations. And there's nothing I can do about it.
Spring is on its way, blood on the table-cloth, an empty
head, my stupid goggling, when I don't feel
like getting up, when I don't know why I should.

**11**

I don't know how much longer I'll be able to take it. No matter
how many boys you bring to me, there isn't one I want to keep.
I can't handle their flapping hands, their loudness,
their clumsiness. I am in constant fear that
they will burst. When they close the door, I am relieved.
It seems that it is out of duty that you lie here
beside me. It is late. It's always late. As we fuck,
the dog's split head appears on the pillow next to
mine. It cuddles up to me. A blue
eye stares at me. I shake and scream,
you think that it is from pleasure. With my fingers
I touch the still warm body, soft hairs.
With teary eyes I look at you
as you vault on top of me with your joyful
smile because you think I'm enjoying it.
You don't understand anything. When you
finish up, the head disappears and I feel
so alone.

**12**

He said that he was sixteen years old and that
he had been fucking around for years. Basically, he didn't know
what to do with himself. He sprung himself on me,

was all over me, licked me, opened to me.
He didn't like aggressiveness, though he bragged about
the fights he'd get into. He stole, robbed, cheated,
surrendered himself to every drug and had great difficulties in
climaxing. While groundbreaking historical events
were taking place in society, he didn't even know
how to read. What would he do with all of my
books? He'd be great on the front line,
he'd shoot like crazy. It would be impossible for
him to ever love. It's all a thing of the past
in any case. I think that all my
acquaintances are together because nothing else
comes to their minds. The years of one's life must be
filled up in one way or another. Sometimes, for no
apparent reason, he'd lie down on the floor in the
corner, curl himself up like a fetus and refuse
to speak to me. Or he'd whisper how much he
loved me. He'd do the least amount of damage, were he to die.
I flinched when I thought about it.
Even more about helping him.


## 13

After the court poets came the wise poets, then the scholarly ones,
the poet seers and then the insane poets. What has now
evolved from all of this are stoned poets.

Not those who sway with their bottles along the
dark streets, frightening cats and breaking their
heads. Just drug experts. They throw themselves onto
the other side, take notes on hallucinations or
pierce their skin. A tattooed hand touches
electronic keys, every so often takes a
straw and sniffs a white line.
When I've had enough, I join you in bed.
You clench your teeth, my head, pull my
hair and push me lower. I stall, so you
go into a rage. You probably feel nothing
towards me, but now you won't let me go.
I sprinkle a bit of white powder over your dick,
you cramp up and explode. What
noise you make! This is definitely not poetry.
Then you turn over, time to get up, because
the life of a stoned poet isn't an easy one.


**14**


Already in the morning it was hot as hell. The kind of day
that stops you. Makes you want to boycott life.
I turned off the radio, TV, telephone, cell phone,
computer, I would even have turned off the fridge so
it wouldn't roar. People's voices
in the rooms next door, outside cars, trains,

bells. I pull the blinds down, so as to at least slightly
block out all the noise, and especially the
sun and heat. By myself, all
sweaty, just like before those basic questions.
A day that I may actually succeed in something.
I move books from one place to another, myself as well,
I don't know what to do with all of this. My head
wants to explode from the pain. And also from the
desire to draw that line across my wrist,
because such a day is exhausting. By myself, I say,
from beginning to end. The hours drag on and
all stands still. I feel like ending all those
feelings that really don't lead anywhere we
were taught. I glance at self-help books about
positive living and can't find the one about
the boycott. A thousand voices repeat *persist,*
*persist,* even though I can tell that
it's pointless. In the past
all is bearable, even beautiful, now this
heat where nothing is right. I close my eyes
and pretend I'm not here.


**15**


After that, I get together with a poet. I am not sure
why. He pulls his manuscript from his bag.

Full of words. I am silent. Actually,
it must be an awkward situation. I watch his
hands turning the pages; perhaps I might caress them.
Though when I travel over his body,
I am not sure whether I am attracted to him
and why this should influence my decision
on his manuscript. He's very smart.
If I were to survey his skin with my
tongue, he'd be saying smart things. I'm taken to a far
away place, he takes out his pipe, which
occupies only moments. As he blows smoke,
I sit with you on the balcony in summer,
the woman from Dubrovnik next to us, we've just
come back, tired, from her bedroom
where we spent hours high on chemicals,
swallowing each other. She says:
a real man should smell of tobacco,
wine and women. She talks and talks
just like this poet, you and I continue
eating each other with our eyes, I feel
you in me. A breeze, all so fragile.
Pages blown across the street, the woman
from Dubrovnik curses her deceased sailor husband,
stones roll into a sea, not at all
promising. Even the poet realizes that I shall
get up and go to the river, look
down and say to myself: I'm nothing.

**16**

Something must be wrong with us. I'm
forty-five years old and I have no one to
think of lovingly. Memories
hurt. I never thought that beauty
could hurt so much. I watch faces and
my breath is taken. Perhaps it's time for me
to dramatically take my own life, or for AIDS to
get me. Whether it's the Seine or the
Hudson, I'm stuck. I go to
suspicious clubs, people talk without
touching, or they fuck in the darkness
of the back rooms without speaking.
All he said was: When we come out, we
don't know each other. Is it better that way? I
look at my feet so as not to fall, I mix up the
streets, here and there small groups of blacks
and their threat, a dread that pulls me,
whether it be Nairobi, Sao Paolo, The Bronx.
I curse my mulatto for being
so impossible, myself, because I still want
something, because there's something wrong with me.

**17**

I read: A fifty-year-old national hero
took off with his twelve-year-old mistress.
I look at the newspaper, despondent. How
could I afford something like that? Ah, if only
I were to take off with that boy from the station
with the dangerous look. Or perhaps if I had
money, I'd buy whichever one I chose.
I'd have an entire harem in my villa.
Or if I had a gun, I'd stick it to
his neck and drag him out
into the dark woods. Perhaps I'd even have to
kill him. But who would notice? It's not
likely that I'd make it to the front page
of the papers. And so, like some kind of loser
I linger in front of the club, I talk to
a fucking sexy Puerto Rican and
try to get through to him that I'm much more
interested in him than his cocaine. He knows how
to put a price on that but not on himself. So once
again, I return alone and I'm relieved
for where would I find the money to
shut him up?

**18**

A young Chinese man explains Derrida to me,
glass in hand he sways. Actually, I'd been
watching him the whole time and wondering what
gender he was. He is shorter than me by
a head, thin, wearing a hat like he'd copied his look from
a gangster movie, he supposedly does write screenplays,
and could pass for a lesbian. Then he steps up to me
and where did he find such a topic,
so feverish. Just ahead in Chinatown,
the Palačinka Bar. I edit scenes, the screenwriter
gets lost, and once again faces walk
along the crowded streets at night. It seems to me
that I've seen this all before, on the screen.
What follows is of course freaks passing by,
retarded, with pockmarked faces
crawling on the ground. Sequences that always
must be cut. I see myself
sitting in the bar and I can't
believe it. The police sirens, firefighters,
flags, the closing credits rolling down fast,
the end and darkness.

**19**

I catch myself constantly checking
my cell for any new messages.
How I'd really love to click on READ
to see the words "I miss you."
I catch myself constantly sinking deeper
into the past, how it lures me back.
To once again be able to lie behind a barn
in the hay when the neighbor boy first
placed his hand between my legs. He was actually
pretending, we both were. He lay on me
clothed, and I could feel his
weight, his panting. How many times
were we drawn up there above the squealing pigs.
Or maybe they weren't, and the barn
already empty. In my memories,
they have become completely unimportant. Our
insignificant moves rose
above it all. It was summer and hot,
we were sweating. We took off our shirts
and undid each other's pants. How
our hands searched and how the hay pricked our skin.
I don't dare stir old memories, but they line
up on their own, the scent of genitals. When
I step into a gay bar, all seems foreign,
no neighbor boy, no hay, no one who misses me.

The entire time I've actually
been searching for the OFF button.


**20**


They didn't give me anything to help me
survive. No faith or hope
to repent, beg, be redeemed. No love
to scatter about. So I wouldn't go on
crashing into things, begging for attention,
tenderness, arms
to embrace me. They didn't give
me old traditions, customs, all the days
alike and I don't anticipate any
specifically. They gave me the ability
to experience pain at the turn of a page, to deal
with it at the same time. With clenched
lips. They gave a rude preciseness
which blows up every so often, causing me
to topple down. They gave me a world
in which I'm staggering and which
I can't feel. I can only see a crowd of
people who've put on t-shirts
that say: *I'm nobody. Who are you?*
We meet in the street, at work, the cinema,
in bars. We talk, ask, answer. And it

hurts. But we don't know any better.

## 21

This miniature Sao Paolo is obsessed with
itself. The swarming heat and the unbearable
human stench convince me that it would be nice
to remain between four walls and give in to
despair. If I still manage to go out with some
acquaintances, the topic of conversation is
where we'll eat. I obviously made
a mistake when I left my home
town where the main question always is: where
and what we'll drink. Actually, there's no question.
From the painful obsession with food and drink
I retreat to an obsession with sex
or something like that, I'm not sure what to call it,
because it's all becoming more abstract. It hasn't become
so bad that I'd spend hours and hours on the internet
for pleasure, but it is disturbing, because I stare at
people for no apparent reason. Perhaps
it doesn't bother them, but it bothers me, I feel
that this habit is becoming an addiction.
A dose of observing beautiful bodies, faces, skin,
I have to increase it each day, fragments appear
to me in dreams, I awake frequently

in a sweat, I'm haunted by cruising streets,
somehow I can't cope anymore. Perhaps I should stop,
using some strong will-power
to give up this behavior. Perhaps I should
admit that I'm addicted, join some
self-help group, or kill
the fantasies in bed with unknown bodies,
sweat, stench, stupid words,
and emptiness.


## 22

I don't know how I ended up in this car. I
went out again, I remember that much, the whole night
I got high and then this guy came
and he just wouldn't leave. I felt his hands
when he somehow led me to the car.
He drove as in a dream, slowly, insecurely,
it seemed to take forever. Maybe a new
day was already dawning. The streets
were empty like a desert, and they were
countless. Then, as though everything was turned off,
I came to my senses in bed. He undresses me and climbs
onto me. He repulses me, yet my hands
are still groping. I avoid his mouth. Like in a spasm,
we cling till it hurts. He gives me a drink and I

slowly come to. He lies on his back, and I
sit on his thigh. From under the pillows he pulls out
a large dildo and hands it to me. He bites his lips
in anticipation. He lifts his legs and invites me
to do it to him. His muscles twitch,
he screams, I try to shut his mouth, but it is
obvious that he likes it. It takes ages.
He changes positions, I look at the wall,
and everything spins. As I become less
stoned, our movements become slower.
Finally, we collapse into silence until it seems
we won't dare look at each other. The view
is of myself stepping down the stairs, losing myself
in that labyrinth of empty streets and not knowing
how I'll find the way from this story.


## 23


Only when thousands of kilometres away from you
do I dare admit that I've fallen in love
with your sperm, with the death that it brought.
I watched it, spilled out over your stomach,
and drowned my face in it. Its scent, which became
the scent of death, brought me
endless orgasms. As though I were using you
for my self-destructiveness. You know it

too, just in a different way. I've
pulled thousands of words from your sperm,
put them to music which held me
on the edge. It seemed to me that I wasn't worthy
and that you'd leave me too.
I couldn't get rid of my father who
didn't think it worthwhile to stand beside me.
That's why I didn't find it unusual when you left me
a thousand times. And each time I
returned to the edge of your stomach with wet
cheeks I lay there waiting for you
to get up and leave once more.


## 24

I don't like going up tall buildings. As long
as I look into the distance, it's ok, but when I
glance down, I feel a dreadful pull. Don't
let me near the brink of a precipice for I'd
surely fall. That's what scares me: I'm afraid of
vanishing. If I think of death, I'm devoured by an
unbearable whirlpool which grabs me by the throat and
steals my breath. With you I hoped to become
accustomed to death, that I would tame it.
When you squeezed my neck during sex,
there was no fear. I could still

see you, I didn't vanish. How unusual
that I should panic at the touch
of other hands that would grab my neck.
Millimeter by millimeter you would tighten the rope.
When one can no longer speak. Maybe you should
tie me up and send me over the edge.
Maybe I should gather the courage to kill myself in one
way or another. It would bring me peace.
Would carry me into nothingness.


## 25


The trip that was truly ours was not to
London, New York, Tokyo or Sao Paolo,
that wouldn't have been wild enough. We
had to go amongst blacks so we could constantly
be afraid, so there was tension, huge
cockroaches, the blood of a dead bison, and lions'
jaws that were tearing up its meat. During the blackouts
in Nairobi, we were barely able to steal away to
our broken-down rooms. That's how it had to be
so we could have only each other, so we were
able to cling to each other like frightened monkeys.
I don't even recall if we gathered up enough
energy for sex. But still, it was all
sex. Birth and death. Stoned children who

aggressively roamed the streets, exhausted
bodies that lay on piles of garbage, uncertain
as to whether or not they were alive, all kinds of soldiers
and buses that got stuck in the mud in the middle
of the wilderness, the sun that rose from
the sea, a remote cinema in which
women smoked, the endless horizon
that makes one dizzy. It would have been better to stay there
in a tent in complete darkness when you pressed up against me
while animals on the roof made mischief.


## 26

He sits in the corner, slouched on a chair, lightly
sways his head to a rhythm, off-beat. He turns
his head towards the ceiling and once again stretches
out his arm towards me, mistily, and again it falls.
Moving bodies hide him from me, then
someone pushes me closer, so that he is
suddenly in front of me, under me, he looks
up and grabs my arm as though he
were drowning. I almost fall, coming
to rest on his knees as he grabs my
head and pulls it towards him so he can
suck on my mouth. It hurts. He doesn't stop.
He fastens on to me like a madman, then suddenly

lets everything go, swings his head back and sets me
free. After a few moments he returns,
tries to get up, moves his lips as if
he wishes to tell me something, but no
voice, only a tongue, rosy, licking his lips
and hissing. I stand up, lift him up
so that he sways dizzily, almost falls, as he leads me
by the arm somewhere outside. I hardly know
how much time passes till we are suddenly in
the car and he takes off my shirt. I see him
above me, completely naked, he is nothing
but mouth, tongue and teeth
devouring my flesh. He whispers incoherently,
rolls his eyes, dozes off, is still, then revives
himself again, is everywhere, floods me. Then,
as though he'd fallen asleep, he lies in my lap
as my fingers comb through his wet hair. Oh, fuck,
if I gave him one more shot, would he die?
What an experience, in my lap! Or even
worse, my deadly kiss! He'd suddenly
be taken, I'd run my fingers over his
smooth dark skin which would gradually turn
colder. In how much time, in how much time?

**27**

He smiled at me in the bookshop from behind
the shelves, his teeth shiny. Of course,
I think, another one hunting intellectuals.
I continue browsing at the letter b, he
already on the other side, perhaps at
m, who knows. Just like in a film, I say to myself,
and he doesn't stop, continues to slide around until
he is right beside me: Excuse me, he grazes me with
his delicious body, he says something else,
but I don't understand. My heart pounds just like
the first time, and by mistake, that's precisely the
book he needs, professionally grabs my arm.
He has won, I want him to understand
that I have no money for sex, but he won't
hear it and invites me to him. I awkwardly
offer lame excuses, after all he could do
anything to me. But it's no go, his skin
is too tempting and when later he traipses past
me, naked, I can't believe it. I stop--
slowly, with hesitation, I take note how he
bites my nipple, then goes lower . . .
to my dick in his mouth. He slides
his rosy tongue around it, sticks it in his
ass and begins to rock on me.
Ashamed, I go on . . . and write

that now he removes the dick and again
devours me as he goes lower until his tongue
is pushed into my crack and with throbbing muscles
he knows he has to fuck me, begins
slowly, constantly faster till the climax as I
grab sweaty black muscles like my life
depended on it. I'm not afraid to admit
that later, when he slept, I was the one
who stepped to the kitchen where knives
hung on the wall and thought that it would have
been best to slaughter him. Staying with him
would be too painful. This way I could more
easily get dressed and leave.


**28**


I dream that I'm a panther. With thick black
fur and bright eyes. I walk behind
you. You turn around and don't dare
quicken your pace, slow down
or stop. I'm bothered by the wide avenue,
the high-rises, the red-hot asphalt,
I'm bothered by the low houses, frightened dogs,
people who jump aside. You sit,
tired, in front of the café, as I lie
at your feet. You wait. No one takes your

order. They watch from afar and
think that it's a performance, that it's a play,
perhaps someone claps, but still they keep
their distance. In the evening, tired, we return
to the house. You spoke to no one, no one gave you
anything to eat, to drink. They watched you
with fear. I rise to my feet
and open the doors. You can't escape.
You lie and would like to die. With my teeth,
I tear off your clothes, lick you with my tongue
as you tremble, hear a siren,
an unbearable noise at the door, human
screams over a megaphone, the whistling of tear gas
cartridges, the smoke rises, I hold you
even closer, I cover you to protect you.
I hear the gunshots, the gunshots.


**29**


Men jumping on top of the bar and taking off
their clothes. Perfected bodies, tanned skin,
muscles. Then again, the ones who scream and shake
their hips, slap your ass, spring back,
mouths twisted into a smile, baring
their teeth. Dancers who stick
injections into their dicks before flying onto

the stage so that for a moment the crowd can't speak
roll out again into a whirlpool of lights
and sweat. My bed is not a medical-examination room, I
say to myself. I want to tidy up the hugs, kisses,
the burdens that have piled up on it. Yesterday
I dressed the wounds of a thin boy who
came to town and injured himself.
Now he throws himself about and shamelessly
goes on about his exploits. Would he understand if
I told him to stop? They often drop by,
those who would debate their own
weaknesses, changes on their skin, cells,
a virus that spreads then disappears.
Or they who tremble for drugs, and have completely
forgotten about sex, altogether impotent.
It would be absurd to say
that people once knew love,
that they could calmly sit on the porch,
and look into each other's eyes, or at the sun as it set,
at the stormy clouds as they approached.
Every so often, they might open a book and read
old texts. I look at prescriptions,
already prepared, already signed, for me
to throw in the trash. The day is so gloomy.
It's Sunday. In the room next door I hear
the sound of those who've just returned from dancing.
I lock the door and lower the blinds.

**30**

Can you hear it, Dave, that noise outside. Maybe
it's a burglar. Or a bomb. Come on, wake up,
Dave, maybe another war has broken out and we'll have
to go into the basement again. You know nothing about this.
How many hours, days, to be spent in darkness.
Or is it only a fire? Has the neighbor fallen out of bed?
Anything is possible. You keep sleeping, not saying
anything. Wake up, Dave, so I won't be alone when
the end of the world comes. You're a pile of meat, Dave, that's
rolled around with everyone. Nothing gets you.
You won't even know when you die and your flesh
starts to rot. It'll be horrible in the basement
and I'll have to throw you to the dogs.
Then all the nightclubs will be safe from you. Dave,
you say nothing. Can you hear me, do you ever listen?
Another noise. I think there won't be
a war. Perhaps it's only our world crashing down
in pieces in the middle of the night when decent people
are asleep, like you, Dave, and I eavesdrop on noises
and am afraid.

**31**

I fell into a depressing reverie on my
uselessness. But still, I'm not a table or a chair or a washing machine,
I said to myself, although sometimes
it seemed that I'd like to be. Let's say
I'd calmly rotate the laundry, thrustingly spin it around
and everyone would be satisfied. Or that bin
in the street, how much garbage is thrown into it. How
many people notice it! Time and time again I took part in
exhibits of useless people. I watched them,
read them, graded them from every angle. This one or that one
would be the right one for me, I'd mumble, although it wasn't
clear to me what I would use him for.
That's why I preferred to be silent and did not approach. But
what's worse was that no one approached me
as though I really were useless. And so we
came and left, always alone, or always more
alone. Every so often I'd meet an old acquaintance
whom I envied because the life he led was completely
different, much fuller, I thought to myself.
I looked at him, surprised, but he just waved his
hand and sadly hissed: it's past the expiration date.
And so he was here again questioning his
uselessness. In such a dim state I
left for the city aquarium. I pressed my nose up
against the glass and watched the fish swimming back and forth.

So calming. Surely, they never desired to be
a washing machine. You truly are a stupid creature, I repeated
to myself.


**32**


As the day grew closer to an end, I felt more
alone. As though the light was meant for
the big wide world, for great self-confident moves. Really,
I always became involved with someone in the evening, or at
night,
in the darkness. As though I were afraid of falling asleep alone.
But it's only sleep; I don't need anyone then.
He might disturb me, push me, steal the covers,
wake me. Countless times I'd bring a boy home in some
great need, incomprehensible desire, to have
him by my side, sometimes even nowhere near my taste,
and then I didn't know what to do about him. How to
get rid of him, or I'd anxiously wait for him to
fall asleep so that everything was calm. Of course the horrid
morning still awaited, especially if I'd been drunk
the night before, sober in the morning. Perhaps I
should face the fact that even my long-term
loves, if I could call them that,
are tied to this, to these evenings and nights. And
did they have the exact same motives? That

they left the world and returned home. An unusual thought.
And I had imagined such extreme commitment,
such deep feelings, unique and once-in-a-lifetime love,
erotic attraction, devotion. Later it always
turned out that it was possible to easily transfer all the
abovementioned things onto someone else. And again there
                    remained
evenings when I was inconceivably drawn to
search again. There were also evenings I felt
that it was all a deception and that there was no escape.


## 33

I am on my way to a poetry reading and standing in front of
a closed door. Some Japanese guy, or whatever he is, tells
me that they'll open in two hours. As though it were
completely normal that nothing is on
schedule. I have no other choice but to go
to the gay village nearby. On the way
in a tacky boutique belonging to an aging youngster, I buy
some sort of a souvenir t-shirt, who knows who it'll be for. But
I've done my duty. I feel like asking him how old he is, but
I wisely refrain. Then I look for the
bar where they've promised a Latino party. Through the windows
I see the aging clientele, no sound or sign
of a party. Finally, I drag myself into a bar

supposedly having a cabaret performance. How fancy.
I look at the guests, even more at the shirtless barman
showing off his muscles. I drink a couple of cocktails,
go to the street twice for a smoke, and look at
his nipples. Yes, I'd take the chest and face,
perhaps a bit Italian, definitely not the hands.
He talks to the guy next to him as though he were putting
on an act, about his holidays or something. I feel dizzy, there's
no cabaret show and I'm no longer drawn to poetry, so
I race to the subway. Good thing there aren't many stops.
I watch the passengers, as always a blend of strange
faces. On the other side, my refection. Yeah, wrinkles, perhaps
I should get an operation. Would that even be appropriate for a
poet? Finally sort of at home on a street with the catchy name:
Manhattan Avenue. Everything sounds catchy here,
just like in Africa where the Hotel Excelsior
is a wooden hut and the New York Bar a stand
next to the butcher's, with huge chunks of meat on hooks
in the sun and swarms of flies. Yes, Gregor,
the neighbor, has once again hung his laundry, like always, on
                    the railing
in the hall. And it stinks because it never dries in
the fresh air. I'm overcome by hunger, devour
greasy sausages so I can gain some weight once again.
On the radio a woman screams about how surprised she is,
what an opportunity, once-in-a-lifetime, and it's like this a
                    hundred

times a day because such opportunities should never be missed.
It's hot on the other side of the ocean. Back home it's now already
morning, and you are surely in someone else's embrace
as usual. There are no messages on the answering machine, who'd
                      bother. Not
even the dog can be thinking about me because remembering is not
in a dog's nature. And so an evening of poetry went to
pieces, not even a poem was made, only banal
prose we might have called immature, hard to classify
as great literature, but how could it be when it is constantly
interrupted by the cat-like howling of police sirens
and the babble of announcers, offering water
on sand.


**34**


I listen to people around me and stare. They have so
much to say, so well-versed, eloquent, wise.
The one in ripped pants goes on about complications
with the town's water supply, the chubby girl next to me about
the constant exploitation of Africa, a third goes into detail about
a new role of I don't know which actor in I don't know which film
now showing. I haven't seen it
which means that all I can do is sink in
shame. An acquaintance sitting next to me suddenly demands
to know what my take is on the crisis in the Middle

East. I go numb. I could have guessed, though, that he'd
want to talk. With great difficulty, I mumble
a couple of sentences and spoil his mood.
Instead of getting into a splendid exchange of
standpoints and views, I stupidly stare, wishing that
he'd stop asking me questions. I open a magazine
to look for classifieds. As though it were the most urgent thing.
So lonely I could place an ad, I say to myself, although
I'm immediately worried about how it would go
and what it would be for. I look over the form I
would have to fill out and am immediately covered in goose-flesh.
My favorite film, favorite book, five things I'd
take with me to a desert island, what kind of partner I'd like,
and, oh
goodness, why I'd be worth meeting. I don't know how to answer
any of these things, as though I've never thought about it or
about
anything. My favourite food, my favourite drink.
No one has ever asked me these things. Never.
Embarrassed, completely incompetent, I close the magazine.
Sadly, I look at the acquaintance beside me, how bored he is,
and hope he'll leave soon and that no one will expect
anything of me. I don't know where I got the idea
I'd been taught to be silent. Everyone around me, especially
grandfather,
constantly worked, words rarely spoken,
only when absolutely necessary. I don't remember anyone ever

debating anything, at least not in my presence. And
no one ever asked me about my favorite food. Or
what I wanted. Even the neighbor boy and I were silent
as we embraced.


## 35

Only two eyes sparkling in the dark and I'm
irrepressibly drawn. As in a hurry, my hands
examine the body, the skin, under the belt, with
my mouth I consume his pouty lips which fill
me completely. Whether on Christopher Street
or Metelkova, he gets lost, and I
eventually wander off amongst the sweaty bodies and
bump into him caressing the hand of some sleaze. As if to say,
my friend's having problems. Hey, fucking black guy,
Slovenian, Frenchman, Bosnian, fuck off, keep your
balls to yourself! Or when he walks by with another
guy, as though it were nothing, or as though I were nothing,
hard to say that he's in his right mind. Days
go by and years, overfilled with words that are
meaningless. I read about one politician shooting another
in the town hall. Now they are both dead.
The insane story goes on and brings naked pictures of
the handsome murderer with a perfect body at a time when
he still frequented the bars, had sex in the toilets

and probably, like you, got lost for hours amongst
the countless dancers. It's a good thing
that I kept my cool and didn't kill you. It would make
all the papers and perhaps my book
sales would increase. In them, I killed you
slowly, piece by piece, and others, the countless
victims of the serial killer within me.


**36**

I watch all these thin boys, posing on the corners,
Chinese, Arabs, Blacks, Latinos, Bosnians, how
they laugh, spit while grabbing their dicks.
I undress them with my eyes: their chests,
their flat stomachs, their dark muscles, the to and fro
of their bodies. How they hurl themselves at the ball,
take their shirts off in the heat until beads of sweat
glitter, whistle at girls, and I imagine how they'd
chase after me if they knew I was watching them.
Their eyes curiously leap into the world,
and it is clear that the worst is over for me, I can
observe them with ease, for what on earth
would they do in my bedroom, where things are
in order, no need to look out for the police, no need
to get excited about fights, or run from gunshots.
What ever would they tell their friends, what would

they brag about, what would lend them glamour, the heroes
of the next block. I find smoothness at the gym
where muscles are on display. Or at the
bars, or on the beaches, where thousands of gay men
race against time. Yet how would they
train in my bedroom, how would they compete, when
time stopped, how would they comprehend tiny
kisses, enjoy silence or a whisper.
The unknown would frighten them, as it did you, who,
smiling, proudly stepped through the door, then
became smaller and smaller until you
vanished in the morning haze.


## 37


You're missing it all, Little Jimmy. Look, a thousand bodies are
waiting for you down there. The techno music makes
                    everything rumble,
muscles tensed, nipples hard, tattooed skin, piece by
piece longing for you, hands inviting, what are you
waiting for? In the back room, labyrinths reek
of poppers, sweat, the walls, you among
the throng as their tense dicks prod you, waiting,
testing to see if you've got a tight ass. Heads hot
from vodka, beer, and coke as you slip on
lubricant, who knows where you step, tongues

stuck into your mouth, your armpits, bellybutton,
ass, Little Jimmy, just spread your legs and a thousand dicks
will fill you up, all will be ecstatic and whoever
asks *Do you have a boyfriend?* will seem stupid to you
for this is a place where protein is drunk, faces are
sprayed, people tied up with ropes deeper in the darkness
in that place for moaning, panting, falling to one's knees,
          licking
boots, this is where everything you've missed and thought
you could live without is. Little Jimmy, where have you
gone to now, why don't you give in to this bliss, why are you
          running away
when everyone is offering you pleasure, happiness.


## 38

I don't know why you came to mind. The first one
I'd ever kissed, though you were too drunk
to know anything about it. But I felt
unbearable pain and happiness, longing only to touch you,
to feel your gaze as I softly caressed
your back. I don't know if I've ever thought about sex
with you. I've never quite pictured it.
It all began that time you wanted to drive me around on your
          bike.
I'd love to be your girlfriend, I thought to myself, because I

didn't know any different. You took care of me, spoiled me,
                        wanted
us to get together in the evenings alone to hold hands and blush.
Then everything turned around. Look, because you didn't like these
feelings, you've become a fat, boring man. If you ever
remember me, you probably get sick to your stomach. And
thanks, because otherwise I wouldn't be sitting in the laundromat
waiting for clothes to be washed while outside it's raining,
some Chinese jumping around, the machines rumbling.
I read the poems of Killian and don't realize years are thrusting by.
Every so often I try to go back, as though
it were possible, and find a teenage boy who loved
to give me a ride, take hold of my hand.


## 39


It really appears as though I'll be joining those who write
at airports, on planes, on trains, who incessantly follow
words, not their thoughts. The chaotic world pours in
from all sides, and high above it, these pages may be
a few hours away. A young woman sits next to me, and I'm
                        bothered
by the feeling that she may want to have a conversation.
Why this feeling of threat? An observer of the world. First she
                        reads psalms,
a bit in English, more seriously in Hebrew. Then she flips

through Cosmopolitan, maybe she wants to be famous, and on
                        the tv
she opts for some tacky American show, no dinner, she has
dry bread and water with her. If we fall down, she'll hungrily
go to God-knows-where. I read, hiding myself in a book about
                        Colombian
boys who kill and love. On the screen I prefer
hairy beasts, foxes, bears. I'd like to be a
sea horse, that yellow kind, I'd carry thousands of young
in my stomach and then spit them out, each to its own
fate. It all becomes so hopeless when things are less to
your liking, less people, less words. You are silent.
And this flight in no way resembles that of a bird.
Or I'd be a migratory bird, always on the move, never
tied down to one land, to one nest, to one bird, what
bird, if I could fly, the erotic would fade away.
Oh, now she's pulling out Agatha Christie as if things
weren't already a horror show. The screaming of children, the
piercing siren of babies crying. I don't know why I'm not
                        allowed to bring
a dog onto the plane, it would surely be less noticeable than
                        these human puppies.
Perhaps one of the wings has been torn off and we're being
                        carried, carried away.

**40**

Beloved Ana, Ljubljana is a nightmare. The first
thought that comes to your mind is to cut
your wrists, to tie a noose, or to leap
from a building. You'd have to be constantly drunk or stoned
to take it. Friends aren't friends, acquaintances aren't
acquaintances, lovers aren't lovers, a mother isn't a mother,
a father isn't a father, a wife isn't a wife, the ground isn't the
                          ground,
all hovers in the never-ending emptiness, hallucinations, ghosts,
freaks, water isn't water and air isn't air, fire isn't fire.
Beloved Ana, your city is the end of the world
without any form of hope, it's vegetating, it is
torment, it is a pinching in your stomach, a concentration
of all the negative forces doing everything in their power
to make an idiot out of you, a cripple. Ljubljana,
the sweet-sounding snake that wraps itself around your body,
softly, with feeling, so you run out of air and can't get rid
of her, always follows you, slithers after you,
so colorful and un-dangerous. Disappear, plunge into
the swamp, return to the mud, forever,
save us.

**41**

Grandfather was the first who realized that I'm not worthy
of life. My bawling got on his nerves so much
that he locked me in the pig-sty. Perhaps the pigs
would have crushed me, an infant, had I not been
saved. I was saved the second time when I
tumbled into the stream, face down in the mud and
suddenly no air. They pulled me out by the
legs. The third time, grandfather again, from the top of the house
where he was repairing the trellis, supposedly by accident
                    dropped
a sharp stick on my head while I was looking out
the window. I stepped back into the room and
watched the blood flow from my head while standing. I didn't
feel a thing. The puddle on the floor grew larger and
larger until someone came along by chance.
Then memory becomes foggy, the only thing that remains is
that I told the doctor that I'd banged my head
against a wall. I should have died. At least three times,
if not more. Then they murdered me, slowly, year
after year, so I got used to it, and waited
apathetically for them to succeed just once. You made
the most effort. You strangled me, stopped me from breathing,
                    broke
my bones, ravaged my brain. More than a thousand times
we had sex, and each time you watched to see whether or not

I'd overstep the boundaries and never return.
No one saved me any more. And it was so
difficult. What killed me even more was when you
fucked others beside me, breathing heavily and screaming
you could never get enough, like you had thrown
me into a pigsty. You killed me the most when you brought
my dog, who had been run over, in your arms, slowly, like in
a movie, like the last sequence, then darkness.


**42**


I don't understand why everything is so wrong. Let's say
it's 7am and I'm driving home from an all-night party and I'm
                    stopped
by two cops who haven't finished school yet, walking over
like a couple of cowboys, accusing me of everything
so I can only wonder what I'm doing in this country as I step
on the gas and drive off. My ex-wife calls hysterically,
asks why I've been harassing, stalking, spying
on her all these years, I should just find myself a woman
already, there are enough of them, that I should just
stop, stop, stop. My guy begs me to hate him,
turns away, then pushes me, keeps on playing me
songs like Depression In the Eyes and Nice Day For
Death. I don't understand what he wants to tell me. When
I retreat to be among people, their mixture

of downers, uppers, and alcohol pulls me like
a whirlpool down to where I am constantly
nervous and can't calm down. I live
in the most stressful town in the world. I try to
pull myself together, but my hands are shaking. I get scared
and they shake even more. I think about where
I could escape to, in what city I'd hide. It seems to me
more and more that my life is nothing but strung-out dreams of
escape.


**43**


I went to see my doctor and admitted
with embarrassment that I had no will to live. I don't know
how I came to this point, as though I had never
had it, or as though I never knew what it was. I observed
my family, each member separately, then my friends
or acquaintances or co-workers, or everyone I had
ever met and no one seemed to have the will to
live. She said I should find a hobby, and I immediately
countered by asking her if she had a will to live.
She smiled sourly and looked at my
file: We aren't talking about me, but about you,
there must be a thousand things that make you happy. That
means nothing, and do they really, truly?
Just calm down, she concluded, there is absolutely

nothing wrong with you, this is something completely normal, it
will pass just as it came. And I couldn't recall
when it came, that it would pass in the end I didn't
doubt. Tired from her treatment, I returned
home. I looked into your eyes. I no longer saw
anything, there was nothing there. Only the dog gave
obvious signs that with him it hadn't yet passed.


**44**


The nights are long and do not bring sleep. I lie in darkness
listening to each sound, and when footsteps can be heard,
I become nervous, wondering if they'll be followed by the
                    rattling of keys.
Then the darkness calms down, images are strung up, and
                    again new
sounds. So it goes the entire night, short scenes of passionate
dreams, I feel my skin, my body, waiting for you.
When, in the middle of the night, the footsteps do irrepressibly
                    approach,
my heart beats faster, the doorknob is moving. I see
how you shift in your drunkenness as though you don't know
                    where
you've come to. You undress and lie down beside me. Nerves by
                    then
have calmed, all at once, when I lay my head down on your

chest, and it's all over. You mumble: Why on earth are you
still with me? You get nothing from me! I am silent.
You want an answer and are drunkenly begging. I press up
against you and can't fall asleep like this. The night is
long. The journey has begun. You are on the edge, retreating
from me in your sleep, and I crawl toward you, behind me the
                    dog
presses up against me, so that half the bed is completely
empty. Such is our journey and no one understands anything.


**45**


As we fly over the clouds, I think: it would be best to fly all
the time. The sun always shines here. It's so peaceful, although
the plane could explode in a moment and goodbye life. I weigh
in my hand an anthology of contemporary American gay poetry. I
can't make the decision to open it. I surely don't belong in
it. In my other hand I hold an essay about new trends in
                    contemporary
Slovenian poetry. It seems to me that I won't be able to
find myself in this either. I pretend that all is normal, even
                    though
it isn't. American poets are envious of my position, not being
one of many. Slovenians are embarrassed, stuffy,
preferring to keep quiet. I suspect it has something to do with
                    fear. This

can sometimes be linked to envy. They never succeed in
getting hundreds of people into the streets. And not for ideas
that will die. They are never around then, and that
says a lot. But still, all these dilemmas are futile.
This struggle of theirs to be mentioned in history is absurd.
I don't feel like reading, as though it were in a foreign language. I
watch the clouds, how they accumulate, swarm and push,

        white clouds

offering a soft ground for one to step onto
and lie down on. This is how angels were invented.


## 46


She caught me. Right in the middle of a James Schuyler poem.

        Not

that there's anything special in the poem. I flinch. I am waiting
for a flight to Sweden and she sits next to me. I sense her

        fidgeting.

Not even a minute passes and already she asks me what I am

        reading. She

doesn't hesitate. I turn the book over so that she's hit by the

        greasy title,

gay poetry. What else should I have done. Ooooo, she howls.
I interrupt her and ask her a few pointless
questions. Yes, she's American and is going to get married this

        very

weekend. I shift my eyes to the book. I had been looking right
                    past her
in any case. She waits a bit, so as not to be so obvious, then she
stands up and goes somewhere else. I am angry with myself.
                    Because
I felt that uneasiness within me. For decades I haven't been able
to get rid of it. I'd really like to tear the book's cover off.
And why that word: *caught?* A notorious author of gay
literature, now a child again, hidden under the blanket
I held a flashlight to the drawings in a children's story.
The shirtless boys playing on the beach. The main hero
was especially to my liking, his slim tight body.
How stupid that tension of mine, the pounding of my heart, for
who would ever figure out that I don't look at girls but
boys. It's hard to put an end to it, the blushing, the trembling.
I close the book and go to the washroom. As I stand at
the urinal, dick in hand, the thought runs through my head
                    again.
I look ahead in the dark and I don't dare look to the left, nor to
                    the right.
I feel guys on either side, I hear the whizzing, surely as
always checking each other out. Comparing. And I, stiff,
petrified that I'd be caught. What a weight they
burdened me with! The boys are whipping it out – and I've
                    been excluded
from this game. Because I really mean it? Because I read gay
literature? They'd known for ages and never invited me

to their games when they'd put someone on display.
Even now they are somewhat ill at ease. As I am because
of them. That is why I rarely read in public,
I socialize with people as little as possible.
As though I am embarrassed to exist.


**47**


The Vietnamese woman will defeat my words, her manuscript on
silk paper, like tiny drops of blood. And as she reads to
me, I hear the rattling of tropical rain. Water
flows, the uncrossable jungle, footprints of soldiers' boots,
film images of forgotten landmines, and sometimes on a sunny
day a distant explosion. She is slender, tiny, like she's crawled
into herself, she looks up from under her brow, instilling fear.
Long black hair, she aimed her animal-like pupils
straight at me. From the distance, the past, barely from
memory, an unexpected twitch, as though I had reached out my
                         arm
and touched her. I undress her with my gaze, lie down beside her,
thrust myself into her and all the trees fall, destroying
houses, she screaming like a beast. It has been years since
I penetrated a woman's body, and I only gaze, astonished:
 where did this image creep in from. She is buried by the avalanche
that rolls down over me, crowds of people, rolling
apples, spent prostitutes who write memoirs,

haughty novelists, bothersome literary agents, names,
names, moose that stray into the city, politicians, police,
soccer players, how they carry themselves, these fictional stars
in a long extinguished sky which as though weeping
for some ultimate phenomenal shooting star that
no one survives.

**48**

You won't believe it, he says to me, in my dreams you
turned into a shapely young man who sells clothes
in menswear at the department store. Every so often
he looks at himself in the mirror and customers thirstily
look him over. They try on pants, sweaters, they keep
coming back and asking strange questions. Friends
come to say hi, a girlfriend waits for him after work, so
they go to a nearby bar for a drink. He smiles
and obviously has no worries. When he gets
drunk, he lets people touch him, and his girlfriend
pulls away. And once, you say, I pulled
him into the changing room, to look into his blue
eyes. And then? I ask. Nothing. I came home and
you were putting away the dishes, the laundry, you
kept on organizing some papers and I couldn't
share my dreams with you. Then at the table
you get up and leave. You always leave when we reach

the beginning of a conversation. Really, perhaps it would be
                    better if I sold
clothes, the world would be so simple and you would dream
about me again, how I was once someone else.


**49**


I march past the parked cars as twilight falls onto
the town. Loud music emanates from one, and two
shadows. She with long hair bows to him.
Embarrassed, I look away, remembering
similar tendernesses. Afterwards, a gentle scream.
Curious, I turn around, I see a hand, hitting her,
twice, she doesn't even budge, doesn't leave.
Confused, I hurry on as though I've been frightened,
as though I can see myself. How hard it is to get rid of these
gestures. As a child, you would cringe to avoid the threatening
                    hand,
as a grown-up you threaten with it. I am ashamed a
                    thousandfold and
that scene in the car which seemed to me a lost
romance was no more than forgotten violence. Who shall I
blame for that? For not knowing how to resist.
At home I crawl to you, as though I want to redeem myself with
someone. You've curled up into a ball and know nothing.
You prick up your ears, you open your eyes and look at me.

I stroke your head, quietly sing to you like to a child
a lullaby, the city is loud, filled with parked
cars, but just go to sleep, go to sleep.


**50**


To forget how a wounded deer strayed into our
corn field and grandfather called the hunters to take her
away. So small, weak.
To forget about the boys who had their secrets and hid
them from me. Whenever I'd ask them about it,
they'd say: you're still too little. I was always
still too little and I never did find out what they'd done.
To forget about the boy who fell in love with me in kindergarten
and kept kissing me while the teachers just
smiled: But he's not a girl!
To forget the vague shuddering, the fever that
flooded my body when my classmates, one after the other,
came over to my house. I tutored them because they
had bad grades, and in class they'd agreed that I'd
be just the right one to help. The boys shared me,
the girls shared a girl from the class.
To forget how my eyes strayed to their first facial hair,
how in gym class I preferred to pretend I was sick so
I could sit on the bench and watch

them chasing the ball.

To forget my first writings that were intended for these boys.

To forget my desperate drunkenness because then and only
then did I dare touch my first love.

To forget everything that came afterwards.

To forget my first girlfriend who never gave it up even
though I constantly tried. Unbelievable how
horny I was then!

To forget the man who, misled by my long hair
and thin body, called to me on the school steps
and when I turned around he undid
his old-fashioned coat and showed me his
ugly red dick.

To forget the feeling of disgust that stirred in me, and the
tenderness with which I looked into my classmate's blue eyes.

To forget the time when I turned my back on the world of men
and towards a wife who had helped me with this. Our
wonderful
stay at the seaside when it seemed that
life was but ocean waves.

To forget my step-father's mawkishness that constantly
threatened me
so that I retreated, for I was afraid that his
touches wanted to be something more.

To forget nothing rolls off my tongue, that many things
won't roll off my tongue and I prefer to hide, be silent, prefer
to forget. Ah, Joe Brainard, better to forget,

forget everything, because it keeps touching the painful raw
                              spots,
and it won't stop till death. To forget, to forget.
At times in my room, there's a horrible silence
and an even more horrible darkness.

**BRANE MOZETIČ** (Ljubljana, 1958) has published twelve volumes of poetry, two novels, and a short story collection. He has also edited three anthologies, and has translated numerous authors from the French including Rimbaud, Genet, Foucault, Guibert, Dustan, Cliff, and Brossard.

He has been awarded the City of Ljubljana Poetry Prize and the European Poetry Prize-Falgwe, among other honors.

His books in English include *Butterflies* (Spuyten Duyvil) and *Passion* (Talisman House) and the forthcoming novel *Lost Story* (Talisman House).

English translations of his poems have been published in *Poetry International, Talisman, Transcript, Verse, Prague Literary Revue, Chroma,* and elsewhere.

For many years he has been active in civil social movements and a leader of the gay movement in Slovenia. He lives in Ljubljana, where he directs two literary collections (Aleph and Lambda) and is director of the Center for Slovenian Literature.